Elegant Eating
in
Hard Times

CW00607094

Elegant Eating in Hard Times

VEGETARIAN MAIN DISHES

By Gloria Withim

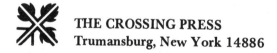

THE CROSSING PRESS
Trumansburg, New York 14886

For Phil, Brockett, Alma and Jocelyn for enduring
Black Bean Soup.

Cover design, Mary A. Scott
Cover photograph, Brockett Withim
Book design and typesetting, Martha J. Waters
Illustrations, Janice Angelini, Penknife Studios

Library of Congress Cataloging in Publication Data

Withim, Gloria.
    Elegant eating in hard times.

    Includes index.
    1. Vegetarian cookery.   2. Low budget cookery.
I. Title.
TX837.W57 1982   641.5'636   82-14916
ISBN 0-89594-087-6
ISBN 0-89594-086-8 (pbk.)

Acknowledgments

I would like to thank:

My students over the years for their enthusiasm and encouragement and for their willingness to explore new recipes and help in their evolution.

Pat Rom and Bill Eschelman for years of good conversation about good food, for helpful advice about books and especially for encouragement and such, through all my stages of development.

Jean Free of Jay Garon-Brook Associates for her warm faith in my manuscripts, and for introducing me to Elaine Gill of The Crossing Press.

My husband, Phil, without whom this book and my career could never be.

Contents

To Begin With . . .

Most of us are conscious of serious problems with our food. They are reflected in the burgeoning prices at the supermarket, in the increasing articles on the dangers of additives, in the dire warnings of food shortages. It is shocking to realize that it takes two acres of arable land to feed the average American while across the world less than a single acre is available per person. Since it requires about seven pounds of grain to produce one pound of meat, the more directly we consume the protein derived from grains and vegetables, the more efficiently we employ that one acre of arable land available in the long run to each of us.

One way to alleviate such problems is to alter our eating habits. We can, for example, recognize that we don't need meat at every meal. The various grains and certain animal products, such as milk, eggs and cheese, contain the necessary proteins for a balanced diet. In many cases, these proteins are more easily digested and more fully used by our bodies than the very solid and highly caloric proteins derived from meat. Such fare need not be dull or uninviting. Quite the contrary.

The cornerstone of quality cooking wherever one lives is fine ingredients. Finding them isn't always easy but the time invested has many rewards. I've come to treasure my frequent trips to an early nineteenth-century mill for unadulterated flour, to a local cheese factory that provides magnificent cream and unsalted butter as by-products, to an Amish egg farm nestled in an exquisite valley and a weekly Farmer's Market featuring local produce not suffocated in tight plastic wrappings. A small garden plot can yeild satisfying quantities of fresh herbs and hard-to-obtain vegetables such as arugula, sorrel, salsify, shallots, leeks and chayotes with a minimum of effort and soil requirements. Otherwise unobtainable ingredients can be mail-ordered or gathered on your travels. Our frequent visits to relatives in New York always include stops in Chinatown and Greenwich Village to keep our kitchen supplied. Food and cookware shops around the world always tell you a great deal about the life styles of the local inhabitants.

In these recipes I have used fresh produce for better flavor. While canned and frozen vegetables do save preparation time, we pay for it through increased costs, less nutrition and less flavor—surely a poor exchange. I employ herbs generously for they not only enhance flavor but also contain valuable nutrients in a form more potent and accessible than the ubiquitous vitamin pill.

My family and friends have enjoyed these recipes over many years. We find our health and our enjoyment of food to be significantly better than when we ate meat daily.

I have known since childhood that good eating is one of life's few real pleasures, an attitude easily indulged in metropolitan areas with their range of restaurants, elegant bakeries and fancy food shops. However, in rural areas like my small central Pennsylvania town, we must develop our own resources, not such a bad idea, really. An hour or two in the kitchen can result in a bountiful table to share with family and friends in the most congenial of atmospheres. Exploration of different foods and cooking styles can bring us into intimate contact with whatever culture we choose no matter where we happen to be.

Stocking The Pantry

I frequently mention herbs, spices and ethnic ingredients throughout the recipes that follow. Below is a list of the more unusual ones, where you may buy them and other useful information. Alternative names are given in parentheses.

BEAN CURD (Tofu): Made from soy beans. An excellent source of protein. Available in many supermarkets, health food and oriental stores. Almost no flavor of its own, custard texture. Beware of added preservatives in some brands.

BEAN THREAD (Cellophane Noodles, Vermicelli): Also made from soy beans. Available in oriental shops.

CHILIES: Fresh green, pickled small (jalapeño) and dried red. Seeds are more intense than the flesh. Handle with care since they will burn the eyes or even the hands occasionally. Fresh chilies can be frozen whole in a plastic bag and will thaw in minutes, losing only a little flavor and texture. They may also be dried by stringing on thread and hanging for a week in a cool place. Some kinds of chilies are usually available, but Tabasco sauce or cayenne can serve as a substitute.

CHUTNEY: Sweet-sour, spicy pickled fruit mixture. An accompaniment for curries, it is available in specialty shops and sometimes fancy food sections of supermarkets. Not difficult to make, however.

CILANTRO (Coriander): Similar to flat-leaf parsley but more pungent. Fresh leaves available in Hispanic and Oriental markets. Very easy to grow.

COOKING CHEESES: Good varieties are generally available in many supermarkets. Grate and slice cheese when very cold, but serve at room temperature for fullest flavor. Types: *Cheddar (sharp), Feta (Goat), Mozzarella, Parmesan* and/or *Romano, Swiss.*

CUMIN: Important seed for chili dishes and curries. Ground cumin generally available while whole seed is usually available only in specialty shops or health food stores.

CURRY: Spice mixture used in Indian, East African and Southeast Asian cooking. Varies considerably in flavor and fire. The basic spices are cumin, coriander, cayenne and turmeric. However, clove, cinnamon, fenugreek seed, mustard seed, cardamom seed and other spices are frequently added. Commercial brands each have different combinations, but it is easy to experiment and make your own.

DRIED LEGUMES: Good protein source. Varieties are: *chick peas (garbanzos), pea beans, green and yellow peas, red and brown lentils, pinto beans, red kidney beans, french green haricot beans.*

EGG WHITE: Good source of fat-free protein. Use raw, beaten into salad dressing. Hard-boiled and chopped for salad or soup garnish.

GINGER ROOT: Use minced fresh root for a more solid flavor since the ground doesn't hold up well during cooking. Generally available in supermarkets in the fruit and vegetable section.

HERBS: Dried leaves of aromatic plants, most easily grown. Perennial plants are noted with a (p). If fresh leaves are used, double or triple recipe quantities. Can be grown indoors on very sunny window sills during the winter. Most used are: *basil, bay leaf, dill, marjoram (p), oregano, sage (p), tarragon (p), thyme (English, p).*

MISO PASTE: Made from soy beans, an excellent source of protein. Use as a broth base in place of bouillon cubes. Available in health food and oriental shops.

MUSHROOMS, DRY BLACK: Intense flavor useful as a truffle substitute when combined with fresh mushrooms. Must be soaked in warm water before use. Never use canned mushrooms since they have barely any flavor and an unpleasant texture. Dry mushrooms are available in specialty and oriental shops.

MUSTARD, DIJON STYLE: Imported French mustard paste with distinctive strong taste.

PARSLEY, FLAT LEAF: Always use fresh leaves since the dried version has almost no flavor. Store leaves loosely in plastic bag in vegetable bin of refrigerator. Curly leaf, which is more bland, is available in supermarkets year-round. All types stay green in the garden through light frost and live two years.

PIGNOLI: Imported pine nuts used in Middle Eastern, Chinese and Italian cooking. Good source of protein. Available in specialty shops but usually cheaper in oriental groceries, though still somewhat expensive.

SESAME OIL, CHINESE: Strong, nutty flavor. The oil sold in health food shops is flavorless.

SESAME SEED: Add to salads and breads for additional protein and pleasant texture.

SPICES: Allspice (ground and whole), cinnamon (ground and whole), mace (outer covering of nutmeg), mustard seed, nutmeg.

SUNFLOWER SEED: Shelled, unsalted, a good protein addition to salads. Can be toasted and salted for a snack Mexicans call Pepitas. Available in health food shops, occasionally in supermarkets.

VEGETABLES, FRESH: Those containing more than 12 grams of protein per edible pound are: lima beans, collards, corn, broccoli, Brussels sprouts, peas, dandelion greens, kale, turnip greens, parsley.

VINEGAR: Wine vinegar is more subtle than distilled or cider vinegar. Some additional flavors that are becoming popular for salad dressings and nouvelle cuisine sauces are raspberry, walnut and various herbs, especially tarragon. Fancy vinegars are expensive, available only in specialty shops, but good red wine and champagne vinegars can be found in most supermarkets.

WHEAT GERM: Excellent nutritive value. Sprinkle as a topping on casseroles, soups and salads; add to the batter of pancakes and bread. Available in supermarkets, but avoid brands with honey added since it limits the usefulness of the wheat germ.

WINES AND LIQUEURS: Always choose a cooking wine of drinkable quality. A poor wine will give a raw, rough or bitter taste to the finished dish. Dry red and white wines are useful to have on hand for adding to sauces, soups and casseroles. Be sure to test bottles that have been opened for some time before adding to a dish since wines do turn sour. However, double distilled wines such as sherry, madeira and vermouth do not turn, nor do liqueurs. Useful wines and liqueurs to stock are: *amaretto (almond), brandy or cognac, creme de menthe, dark rum, dry sherry or madeira, triple sec or cointreau (orange).*

Mail Order Sources

APHRODISIA, 28 Carmine St., New York, N.Y. 10301
All manner of herbs and spices. Annual catalog $2., refunded on first purchase. A marvelous herbal with many interesting recipes.

CHEESES OF ALL NATIONS, 153 Chambers St., New York, N.Y. 10007
Free catalog. Many other items besides cheese.

COMPLETE FOOD CATALOG by Jose Wilson and Arthur Leamon, Holt paperback, $6.95.
Varied and comprehensive, extremely useful.

KAM MAN FOOD PRODUCTS, INC., 200 Canal St. New York, N.Y. 10013
Every oriental food product and utensil known to exist available at supermarket prices.

KITCHEN BAZAAR, 4455 Connecticut Ave. N.W., Washington, D.C. 20008
6 catalogs annually with extensive sale announcements. Kitchen equipment and a full line of spices and herbs.

LE JARDIN AU GOURMET, West Danville, Vt. 05873
Imported foods and plant seeds, also potted herbs.

LEKVAR-BY-THE-BARREL, 1577 First Ave., New York, N.Y. 10028
Annual catalog. Spices, herbs, imported utensils.

MANGANARO'S, 488 Ninth Ave., New York, N.Y. 10018
Annual catalog of imported Italian foods. It is also a restaurant, around the corner from the Port Authority, in a neighborhood of street stalls and shops with foods of every nationality.

PAPRIKAS WEISS, IMPORTER, 1546 Second Ave.,
New York, N.Y. 10028
Annual catalog. East European imported foods,
cookbooks, cookware and oddments.
SULTAN'S DELIGHT, 409 Forest Ave., Staten Island,
New York 10301
Catalog. Middle Eastern importer of foods, spices,
utensils, cookbooks, belly dancer costumes, etc.
TUSSEYVILLE TRADING POST AND HERB FARM,
Box 111, Centre Hall, Pa. 16828
Herbs: seed, dried, potpourri, plants, etc.
WALNUT ACRES, Penn's Creek, Pa. 17862
Annual catalog. Organic foods of all descriptions.
WILLIAMS-SONOMA, P.O. Box 3792, San Francisco,
Ca. 94119
6 catalogs a year, in full color and very elegant.
Imported foods, cookware and tableware, many
exclusives.

Crepes

Crepes are the French name for very thin pancakes called *crespelles* in Italy, *palacsinta* in Hungary, *blintz* in Eastern Europe, *dosai* in India and *tortilla* in Mexico. I usually triple the recipe given here, using five skillets at once. Packed by the dozen in plastic bags, crepes can stay in the freezer indefinitely. They thaw in minutes, so handy for a quick and elegant meal. Of the two batter recipes, the first is lighter.

Pan and Technique

PAN: Eight-inch pans made of spun steel, cast iron or enamelled cast iron work very well. I have pans of each material. Cast iron is the least expensive. Spun steel and cast iron pans must be seasoned: scour well with steel wool, wipe clean, add a quarter-inch vegetable oil and heat about five minutes. Turn off heat and allow pan to cool with oil overnight. Next day, discard oil and wipe the pan clean. Never use soap or detergent. Instead scrub with salt when necessary. These pans will need reseasoning periodically.

TECHNIQUE: The thinner the crepe, the better. Very lightly grease pan and heat through. Lift pan off heat. Hold it at an angle. Pour in a large spoonful of batter while constantly rolling the pan to distribute the batter thinly and evenly. Continue rolling pan until batter has completely set. Cook over moderately high heat on both sides. Remove to cool on wire rack. Stack completely cold pancakes by the dozen and wrap in plastic for storage in refrigerator or freezer.

17

Basic Batter

1 3/4 c. unbleached flour
2 eggs
2 c. milk

Place flour in mixing bowl and make a well in the center.
Break eggs into well, beat with wire whisk, gradually incorporating the flour. Add milk, half cup at a time, whisk-
ing all the while. An electric mixer may be used. Allow
to rest and settle one hour before using. Batter should be
the consistency of heavy cream. If it is too thick, add a
little milk. Cook as directed above.
   Unused batter may be kept in the refrigerator for
several days. Cooked pancakes may be kept in the refrigerator for several days and in the freezer indefinitely.
Makes 32-37.

Whole Wheat Batter

1 c. whole wheat flour
2 T. soy flour
1/4 c. stone ground cornmeal
1/4 c. unbleached flour
2 eggs
2 1/4 c. milk

Combine all dry ingredients in mixing bowl and make a
well in the center. Break eggs into center and beat
smooth, gradually incorporating flours. Gradually beat
in milk. Mixture should be the consistency of heavy
cream. Let rest for one hour. Thin if necessary with additional milk. Cook as directed under TECHNIQUE (p. 17).
Makes 26-30.

Filling No. 1
Mushroom and Onion

1/4 c. butter
2 c. sliced onion
1 finely-minced clove garlic
1/2 stalk celery sliced thin
2 1/4 c. sliced fresh mushrooms
1 t. marjoram
1 T. minced fresh parsley
salt and pepper
3 T. dry white wine
12 crepes
white sauce (see Appendix)

Melt butter in 10-inch heavy skillet over moderate heat and saute onions, garlic and celery about 5 minutes. Add mushrooms, herbs and seasonings and saute until cooked through, about 4 minutes. Add wine, cook another 2-3 minutes. Place about 1/3 c. filling in the center of each crepe, roll and place in lightly-buttered baking dish. Coat all the crepes with white sauce and heat about 12 minutes in preheated 350 degree oven. Serve very hot.

GO WITHS: A colorful idea, quite French, is a mixture of cold cooked vegetables such as peas, green and yellow beans, broccoli and cauliflower combined with raw vegetables such as grated carrots, diced cucumber, celery and onion. Toss them in freshly-made mustard mayonnaise (see Appendix).

Filling No. 2
Asparagus/Broccoli/Grean Bean

12 crepes
1/2 recipe mushroom and onion filling (see above)
cheese sauce (see Appendix)
36 stalks asparagus, steamed crisp-tender
    or 24 thin stalks broccoli, steamed crisp-tender
    or 48 trimmed whole green beans, steamed
        crisp-tender

In the middle of each crepe, place 3 stalks asparagus or
2 broccoli or 4 green beans. Add some mushroom filling
to each and roll up. Place in lightly-buttered baking dish,
coat with cheese sauce and bake in preheated 350 degree
oven about 15 minutes to heat through. Serve very hot.

GO WITHS: Grated carrots with minced onion and fresh
parsley, mellowed in a strong vinaigrette dressing for 1-2
hours. Covered in the refrigerator, it will stand well for
several days. If preferred, finely-shredded red cabbage
may be treated the same way. Both are French classics
found in every charcuterie.

Filling No. 3
Ratatouille

> vegetable oil for sauteing
> 1 medium-small eggplant diced
> 3-4 zucchini, 6-inches long, sliced
> tomato sauce (see Appendix)
> juice of 1/2 lemon
> 12 crepes

The amount of diced eggplant should approximately equal
that of the zucchini. Using a skillet large enough to accom-
modate all the eggplant at once, heat about 2 T. oil and saute
eggplant over moderate heat until tender, adding more oil as
needed. Remove eggplant to bowl or plate. Wipe skillet
clean and heat fresh oil. Saute zucchini in same manner.

Preheat oven to 350 degrees. Add eggplant and zucchini with any accumulated juices to oven-proof casserole
with tomato sauce, reserving 3/4-1 c. for topping. Add
lemon juice to casserole and bake 20 minutes. Fill, sauce
and heat crepes as previously directed.

GO WITHS: A tossed salad consisting of several kinds of
greens with shredded red cabbage for color, pine nuts or
sunflower seeds and chopped, cooked egg white for texture and protein. Mix just before serving with a light vinaigrette dressing (see Appendix).

20

Filling No. 4
Aloo Dosai (Curried Potato)

1/2 c. butter
2 c. onion, minced fine
2 cloves garlic, minced fine
1/2 t. fine-minced fresh ginger root
2 t. cumin seed
1 t. mustard seed
4 c. potatoes with skins in small dice
1 T. curry powder
2 t. turmeric
2 t. ground coriander
salt to taste
oil for frying
12 crepes

Melt butter in 2 quart saucepan and stir-fry half the onion, all the ginger, garlic, cumin and mustard seeds until golden brown, about 15 minutes, over moderate heat. Add potatoes and stir-fry another 5 minutes. Add remaining spices with about 1/2 c. water. Cover saucepan and simmer over low heat about 10 minutes. Add remaining onion and continue to simmer until mixture is very tender and there is very little moisture left. Add more water as needed to keep potatoes from sticking to pan. Divide cooked potatoes among the crepes and roll up.

Heat about 1/4 inch oil in a very large skillet. When it is hot enough to toast a bread cube in 30 seconds, add filled crepes, one at a time so as not to cool the oil. Turn each crepe as necessary to fry crisp and brown all round. Remove each as it is done with slotted spoon or spatula to a warm platter lined with paper towels to absorb excess grease. Keep platter warm while the remainder are fried. Serve hot and crisp.

GO WITHS: Instead of salad, serve steamed fresh asparagus or broccoli spears. Since the pancakes do not have a sauce, a coating of cheese sauce sprinkled with toasted sesame seeds would be very nice.

Filling No. 5

Florentine

Dishes containing spinach are often called Florentine in honor of the fine crop grown in Florence.

> 2 T. butter
> 1 c. sliced onion
> 1 c. sliced fresh mushrooms
> salt and pepper
> 1 t. marjoram
> dash nutmeg
> 3 c. chopped, cooked spinach, well-drained
> 12 crepes
> cheese sauce (see Appendix)

Melt butter in 10-inch skillet and saute onions 3-4 minutes over moderate heat. Add mushrooms, cook another 3-4 minutes. Add seasonings and drained spinach. Combine well and allow to cool. Fill crepes, place in lightly-buttered baking dish, coat well with sauce and heat through in preheated 350 degree oven about 15 minutes.

GO WITHS: Sliced fresh tomatoes, in season, with sliced cucumbers and onion rings, sprinkled with basil, salt and pepper. For hot house tomatoes, halve them, season as above and broil quickly.

Filling No. 6

Cheese

1 lb. cream cheese, room temperature
1 c. grated Cheddar
1 c. grated imported Swiss
salt and pepper
1 t. Dijon-style mustard
3 T. minced scallions
1 1/2 T. minced fresh parsley
12 crepes
white sauce (see Appendix)

Combine all ingredients but crepes and sauce in mixing bowl. Divide among the crepes, roll up and place in lightly buttered baking dish. Coat with sauce, heat through about 15 minutes in preheated 350 degree oven. Serve very hot.

GO WITHS: A medley of lightly-steamed peas, green and yellow beans and broccoli, tossed with onion slices and sesame seeds sauteed in butter. Season gently with salt and pepper.

Eggs

Eggs aren't much in favor these days due to their high cholesterol content but this resides only in the yolk which is mostly fat. The white is a fine protein, making meringues quite nutritious in spite of the white sugar. Since many egg dishes do well with some of the yolks removed, I have indicated such reductions where appropriate.

Briyani

This is the Indian version of fried rice. As with most oriental dishes, it is usually made with white rice but I've come to prefer the flavor of brown which is, of course, more nutritious. This type of curry is meant to be mildly spicy but it can be adjusted to your preference.

    1 1/2 c. brown rice
    4 1/2 c. water
    4 bay leaves
    2-inch stick cinnamon
    8 whole cloves
    1/4 c. butter
    1 large onion, minced
    1 t. fresh ginger root, minced fine
    1 t. mustard seed
    1 t. cumin seed

1 c. grated carrot
3/4 c. zucchini in small dice
3 eggs, beaten (may omit 1 yolk)
1 1/2 c. peas, thawed and drained
1 1/2 t. turmeric
salt and coarsely-ground black pepper

Combine rice, water, bay leaves, cinnamon and cloves in a
3-quart saucepan and bring to a boil. Cover the pan and
lower heat. Simmer until water has been absorbed and
rice is tender. Discard seasoning ingredients.

Meanwhile, in a large skillet, melt butter and saute
onion, ginger, cumin and mustard seeds about 15 minutes
over moderate heat until onion is lightly browned. Add
carrot and zucchini. Saute about 3 minutes, stirring
occasionally. Add beaten eggs and scramble lightly into
onions. Remove from heat and add rice along with remaining ingredients. Return to heat and simmer over low
heat 10 minutes, covered, for flavors to combine. Taste
for seasoning and serve quite hot.

GO WITHS: Indian curries are usually served with a selection of condiments such as cubes of fresh pineapple,
sections of mandarin oranges, chopped peanuts or cashews, grated fresh coconut, spicy chutney and hot pick-
les of various types. Add Indian flat bread or pita. Pre-
cede, if you like, with a green salad and finish with an
authentic dessert of custard or fresh fruit.

Gougère Florentine

Cream puff pastry is the easiest of all to make and is most
versatile. With grated cheese mixed in the dough, it can
be served alone or filled for brunch, supper or on a buffet.
Sometimes called Burgundian Pastry in French cookbooks,
it originated during the eighteenth century in the town of
Sens. As indicated, it may be made without egg yolks.

Filling:
- 2 T. butter
- 3/4 c. sliced onion
- 1 c. sliced fresh mushrooms
- salt and pepper
- dash nutmeg
- 2 T. flour
- 1/2 c. dry white wine
- 1 c. chopped, cooked spinach

Pastry:
- 1 c. water
- 3/4 c. butter
- 1 1/2 c. unbleached flour
- 5 eggs (yolks may be omitted)
- 1 c. grated sharp Cheddar
- 3/4 c. slivered almonds

Prepare filling first so it may cool before it is used. Melt
butter in a 9-inch skillet, saute onion about 3 minutes,
add mushrooms and saute another 3-4 minutes. Season,
remove from heat and stir in flour, then wine. Return to
heat, stirring, until mixture thickens. Squeeze spinach
very dry, add to skillet and combine well. Remove from
heat and cool. Mixture should have very little moisture.

For pastry, heat water in a 1 1/2-quart saucepan with butter until it boils and the butter is melted. Remove from heat and add all the flour at once. Stir until an absolutely smooth paste forms. Beat in eggs one by one, incorporating each completely before adding the next. Then stir in the cheese.

Butter lightly individual round or oval baking dishes or a single large dish with sides about 1 1/2 inches high. Shape pastry in a ring around the edges of the dish, fill center with spinach mixture. Sprinkle generously with almonds and bake in preheated 400 degree oven about 25 minutes for individual dishes, 35 for a larger one. Pastry should be a deep golden brown and well-puffed. Can be prepared ahead and reheated.

GO WITHS: For brunch, sections of fresh fruit marinated in a little rum. For supper, either grilled tomato halves or a plate of fresh tomato slices, fruit or sherbet for dessert.

Cuauhtemoc

This is an Aztec dish with a spicy bean base which is perhaps an ancestor of Mexican Huevos Rancheros. Substitute canned refried beans and tomato sauce if you're in a hurry, but a livelier version with better texture will result if you start from scratch.

> 2-3 T. vegetable oil
> 2 minced cloves garlic
> 1 c. chopped onion
> 1 c. cooked pinto beans
> 1 minced fresh green chili
> 3/4 c. chopped, peeled tomatoes
> salt
> 6 eggs
> 1/2 c. grated Cheddar

Heat oil in a 2-quart saucepan. Saute garlic, onion and beans for several minutes over moderate heat about 5 minutes. Add chili, tomatoes and salt to taste. Simmer over low heat about 10 minutes. Mixture should be rather thick but moist. More tomatoes or juice can be added if it is too dry or pasty.

Lightly oil a shallow baking dish. Spread bean sauce over surface, then form 6 hollows with back of spoon. Break eggs into these hollows. Sprinkle generously with Cheddar and bake in preheated 375 degree oven until bubbling, about 20 minutes.

GO WITHS: Make a chunky Guacamole with chopped tomato and avocado, add minced onion, garlic and vinaigrette. Serve on crisp greens, top with crumbled, fried tortillas. End the meal with Flan (Caramel Custard), the national dessert of Mexico as well as Spain.

Oeufs Soubise

This is a handy way to finish off an abundance of Easter eggs. Although this dish is traditionally served on toast, I prefer it on rice.

> 2 T. butter
> 2 1/2 c. sliced onions
> 2 cloves fine minced garlic
> salt and white pepper
> 1/2 t. Dijon mustard
> 2 1/2 T. unbleached flour
> 2 c. scalded milk
> 1/2 c. dry white wine
> 1 1/2 c. brown rice cooked to 3 c.
> 10 large eggs, hard-boiled, peeled and sliced
>   (may omit 3-5 yolks)
> grated Parmesan
> 2 T. minced fresh parsley

Melt butter in a 2-quart saucepan, saute onions and garlic until golden over moderate flame, about 15 minutes. Stir occasionally, do not allow to brown. Remove from heat, add seasonings, mustard and flour. Gradually stir in milk and wine. Return to low heat, stirring constantly until mixture has thickened, about 10 minutes.

   Pile rice on a warm platter or on individual warm dinner plates, arrange egg slices on top and pour over sauce. Sprinkle generously with cheese and parsley.

GO WITHS: Ring the platter or individual plates with still-crisp, steamed spears of broccoli or asparagus.

Omelettes

The rules for a perfect omelette are few and simple. Be sure to beat eggs very well before pouring into hot pan and don't overcook—the middle should still be a little runny. This will produce a light, delicate and flavorsome dish. If you decide to make a filled omelette, prepare the filling before you begin the eggs.

THE PAN: There is little difference between a crepe pan and an omelette pan; the latter's sides slope a bit more to ease removal. Otherwise the same rules about weight and size and seasoning apply (see page 17). Spun steel and cast iron are very porous which prevents an omelette from sticking but they also absorb flavors from other foods which is why omelette pans should be used only for eggs and crepes.

Plain Omelette for Two

4 eggs, beaten until frothy (may omit 1-2 yolks)
2 T. cold water
salt and white pepper
1/2 t. butter

While beating eggs, water and seasonings with a table fork, heat an 8-inch heavy skillet over moderately high heat. Add butter and when it is sizzling, pour in frothy eggs. Stir constantly with the fork but be careful not to scrape the bottom of the skillet and disturb the setting of the eggs. Shake skillet occasionally to keep pan from over-heating. When eggs are well set on the bottom, add filling and heat through. Release all round with the fork and use it to flip one side of the omelette over. Slide out onto a warmed plate, cut in half and eat while still hot and moist.

Filling No. 1

Cheddar and Green Chilies

1 minced green scallion
1 canned green chili, chopped fine
1/3 c. grated Cheddar cheese

Saute scallion in butter about 1/2 minute before pouring in eggs. When bottom is set, add chilies and cheese, fold over and let rest a few seconds for cheese to melt before turning out onto plate.

Filling No. 2

Herb (Omelette Verte)

1 minced green scallion
2 T. minced fresh parsley
1/2 t. chervil
1/8 t. tarragon

Saute scallion in butter about 1/2 minute. Add remaining ingredients to the frothy eggs, combining thoroughly. The mixture will become quite green. Cook as for plain omelette.

Filling No. 3
Mushroom

2 t. butter
2 mushroom caps
1/2 c. sliced fresh mushrooms
2 fine-sliced scallions
2 t. minced fresh parsley
1/2 t. marjoram
1 T. dry white wine

Melt butter in small skillet over moderate heat. Lightly
saute caps about 2 minutes and set aside. Saute remaining mushrooms and scallions with the herbs until tender,
about 2 minutes. Add wine and simmer gently until it is
absorbed. Fill omelette when ready with mixture, fold
over and slide out. Place mushroom caps on top.

Zucchini Omelette

3 T. olive oil
4 small zucchini in thin slices
2 minced scallions
salt and pepper
1 t. oregano
1/2 t. basil
1/2 c. freshly-grated Parmesan
6 large eggs, beaten well (may omit 2-3 yolks)

Heat oil in a heavy 10-inch skillet over moderately high
heat. Saute zucchini and scallions. Add herbs and seasoning. Stir and cook until tender, about 6 minutes. Beat
cheese into eggs and pour into skillet, stirring with fork
until eggs are set. Remove from heat, cut into wedges
and serve from the pan.

GO WITHS: Hot, freshly-made biscuits or muffins in the
morning. Add tomatoes and onions sliced in vinaigrette
(see Appendix) late in the day.

Foo Yung With Brown Sauce

7 eggs, beaten well (may omit 3-4 yolks)
2 stalks celery with leaves, minced
1 large onion, minced
1 c. fresh bean sprouts
1 large carrot, scraped and grated
1/2 large green pepper, seeded and minced
1 c. shredded Chinese cabbage (sieu choy)
1 c. fresh mushrooms, minced
1 T. minced fresh parsley
2 T. dry sherry
salt and pepper
vegetable oil for sauteing
Brown Sauce (see Appendix)

Combine ingredients in mixing bowl. Grease large skillet or griddle with oil and heat over moderately-high heat. Drop large spoonfuls of omelette on skillet and cook quickly as you would pancakes. When bottom becomes lightly browned, turn for other side to brown. Keep warm while remainder are cooked. Serve over rice with brown sauce.

For additional flavor, soy sauce and Hoisin sauce may be added at table.

GO WITHS: Hot, crusty garlic bread and a tossed green salad. For supper, finish with gingerbread (see Appendix) and custard sauce.

Piperade

Scrambled eggs from the French Basque country.

> 2 T. butter
> 12 mushroom caps
> 12 eggs, well-beaten (may omit 4-6 yolks)
> 2-3 T. minced fresh parsley
> Tomato Sauce (see Appendix)

In a large skillet, melt butter and lightly saute mushrooms, about 3 minutes. Remove and keep warm. In the hot butter, scramble eggs quickly. When they are nearly set, stir in tomato sauce very loosely. Mixture should not be homogenous. Serve immediately on warm plates, sprinkling each portion generously with parsley and mushroom caps.

GO WITHS: French fried potatoes, skins on, but sauteed in butter rather than deep-fried. During the first 10 minutes of cooking, keep covered, then remove lid and turn potatoes often with spatula to brown them. Add a salad of cold, cooked green vegetables in a freshly-made mustard mayonnaise and end with a buttery, plain pound cake. (See Appendix for both recipes)

Shirred Eggs With Mushrooms

At our house, Christmas morning always begins with a hearty breakfast of fruit, shirred eggs, a rich stollen and lots of coffee. However, it's too good to eat only once a year. The mushroom sauce is a French classic called Duxelles, used in many dishes and even alone as a canape spread.

> 1 dozen eggs
> 2/3 c. grated Cheddar cheese

Duxelles:

> 1/4 c. butter
> 1 lb. fresh mushrooms, chopped
> 1/3 c. minced scallion
> salt and pepper
> 1/2 t. marjoram
> 2 dried black mushrooms, soaked and minced fine
> 1/2 c. dry white wine

Make the Duxelles by melting butter in a 9 or 10-inch skillet and saute fresh mushrooms and scallion 3-4 minutes, seasoning with salt, pepper and marjoram. Add the soaked and minced mushrooms with their liquid as well as the wine. Simmer gently until moisture has nearly evaporated, about 15-20 minutes. This sauce can be kept tightly covered in the refrigerator about a week and may also be frozen.

Lightly butter individual baking dishes or one large dish. Spread generously with mushroom sauce. Break eggs on top. Cover generously with Cheddar and bake in preheated 400 degree oven 12-15 minutes for individual dishes, 15-18 minutes for one large dish. Bake only until the whites are set. They will toughen if overcooked.

GO WITHS: Crusty rolls, fruited yeast bread, muffins or biscuits are all delicious accompaniments for breakfast or brunch. For supper, add a salad of mixed vegetables in mustard mayonnaise and a dessert of fruit pie.

35

Soufflé

Since souffles are often considered intimidating, here are
some rules for success:
1. Beat egg whites only to soft peak stage. Never
   overbeat.
2. Be sure sauce has cooled enough so that egg whites
   won't melt when they're folded in.
3. Fold beaten whites into sauce-yolk mixture very
   slowly and gently. This step cannot be rushed.
4. Eat the souffle immediately once it is done. Baking
   in individual dishes means less cooking time and
   much easier serving. Pyrex custard cups, stoneware
   soup bowls, any relatively straight-sided, non-metal-
   oven-proof container may be used. It should be
   deep rather than shallow to permit the souffle to
   rise properly.

1/4 c. butter
1/4 c. unbleached flour
2 c. scalded milk
2 c. grated sharp Cheddar
    or 1 c. pureed, cooked carrots seasoned with
        onion, salt, pepper
    or 1 c. sauteed, sliced fresh mushrooms with
        onion, salt, pepper and marjoram
6 eggs, separated (may omit 2-3 yolks)

Melt butter in 2-quart saucepan, remove from heat and
stir in flour, then gradually stir in milk until smooth,
using a wire whisk. Return to heat and simmer, stirring
with whisk constantly, until mixture thickens. Sauce
will be quite thick and pasty. Remove from heat and stir
in grated Cheddar until it melts, or carrot puree or mushroom mixture, depending on preference. Allow to cool
1-2 minutes, then beat in yolks. This portion of the

souffle may be made hours ahead or even the day before. It must be covered with wax paper pressed directly on the surface to gather up the skin that forms.

Beat whites to soft peak stage only and gently fold into sauce. Mixture may be allowed to stand about half an hour. Bake in preheated 325 degree oven, 1 hour for 2-quart casserole and 30 minutes for 8-10 ounce individual dishes.

GO WITHS: A colorful salad of fresh orange and grape-fruit sections mixed with crisp greens, thin onion rings, green grapes or avocado slices, dressed only with a little oil and minced fresh parsley. For dessert, a rich slice of fudgy chocolate cake.

Grains and Beans

Lentils Creole

Lentils are probably the oldest known cultivated food. They lend themselves easily to a variety of seasoning.

1 c. brown lentils
1/2 c. brown rice
1 quart water
2 T. butter
1 large onion, thinly sliced
2 green peppers in slivers
2 c. chopped, peeled tomatoes
salt and pepper
1 t. Dijon mustard
2 t. chili powder
1 t. basil
1 t. oregano

In a 3-quart saucepan, cook lentils and rice in water 30 minutes. Drain. Set aside. They will not be quite tender. Melt butter, saute onion and green pepper until golden. Add remaining ingredients and simmer together about 5 minutes. Add drained lentils and rice. Simmer all together very gently 40 minutes. Add liquid during cooking if necessary. Lentils and rice will be very tender and broth will be thick. Taste for seasoning.

GO WITHS: Crusty hot bread is a natural accompaniment. Add a plate of broccoli vinaigrette and a dessert of cinnamoned baked apples topped with whipped cream.

Cassoulet

One of the most famous dishes of Southern France, Cassoulet is traditionally made with sausage, preserved goose, lamb and pork or ham bones in addition to the ingredients below. This completely meatless version has neither the expense nor the calories while retaining a rich and satisfying flavor.

2 c. pea beans
4 large carrots in thick slices
1 1/2 large onions, coarsely chopped
3 cloves garlic, minced
1 large stalk celery with leaves, sliced
3 sprigs parsley
salt and pepper
1 T. Dijon mustard
3 bay leaves
1 t. thyme
1/4 t. ground cloves
1 1/2 c. dry white wine
2 c. water

Soak beans at least 3 hours in water to cover. Drain beans. Put in a 3-quart saucepan with all remaining ingredients. Cover and bring to a boil. Reduce to simmer and cook very slowly, covered, for about 2 hours, or until beans and vegetables are very tender. Add more water or wine in the course of cooking, if necessary. The finished dish should be quite juicy. Taste for seasoning before serving. May be kept covered in the refrigerator for several days or it may be frozen.

GO WITHS: Serve hot, crusty bread to gather up the casserole juices and a tart salad of fresh orange and grapefruit sections with thin onion rings on lettuce. For dessert, serve lemon or lime chiffon in a crust of ginger snap crumbs.

Indonesian Peanut Rice

Curried peanut sauces are favorites in Southeast Asia and in East Africa. You may increase or decrease the amount of chili according to preference.

2 t. vegetable oil
1/2 c. minced onion
1 t. minced garlic
1/2 t. minced fresh ginger root
1 T. miso paste (soy bean paste)
1 1/2 T. soy sauce
1 t. crushed red chili pepper or to taste
1 t. crushed coriander seed
3/4 c. natural peanut butter, chunk-style
1 T. lime juice
2 c. brown rice cooked to 3 1/2 c.

Heat oil in a 9 or 10-inch skillet, saute onion, garlic and ginger. Stir in miso, gradually add 2 c. water. Add all remaining ingredients but lime juice, blending well. Simmer over very low heat about 10 minutes for flavors to blend. Remove from heat. Stir in lime juice. Serve over brown rice.

GO WITHS: A condiment tray makes an authentic and handsome accompaniment. Arrange small dishes of chopped peanuts, minced raw onion, small cubes of fresh pineapple or mandarin orange slices, cubed fresh tomatoes, cubed ripe avocado sprinkled with lemon to maintain color, shredded Chinese cabbage flavored with 5-spice powder and sesame oil. If you wish dessert, serve fresh fruit or sherbet.

Baked Mushroom Kasha

Kasha (buckwheat groats) is a staple of the Middle East. It is available in bulk at health food stores and in boxes at supermarkets.

> 1/2 c. butter, melted, divided
> 1 c. chopped onion
> 1/2 c. chopped green pepper
> 1 minced clove garlic
> 1 stalk celery, minced
> 1 1/2 c. sliced fresh mushrooms
> 1 c. kasha
> salt and pepper
> 2 c. boiling water
> 3 c. grated sharp Cheddar

Using a wide 3-quart saucepan or a deep, 12-inch skillet, add half the butter and saute the next five ingredients until golden, about 8 minutes. Add kasha and salt and pepper and stir thoroughly. Pour in the boiling water, cover and steam 25 minutes. Water will be completely absorbed and mixture will be quite tender.

Lightly butter a shallow baking dish about 8 x 12 inches and spread the kasha in the pan. Drizzle with remaining melted butter and top with Cheddar. Run under broiler so that cheese will melt.

GO WITHS: Celery cut in thick slices on the diagonal, sauteed in light sesame oil and soy sauce, liberally sprinkled with slivered and toasted almonds. An easy and festive dessert is fresh pears poached 10 minutes in white wine, cooled in the liquid and served with a scoop of raspberry sherbet.

New England Succotash

This is a more elaborate version of the maize dish the Native Americans taught our first settlers.

> 1 c. pinto beans, soaked at least 3 hours
> 1 stalk celery with leaves, sliced
> 1 large carrot in thick slices
> 1 onion studded with 3 cloves
> 1 bay leaf
> 4 sprigs parsley
> water to cover
> 2 c. cooked corn
> 2 T. butter
> 1/2 c. onion, sliced
> 1/2 c. green pepper, diced
> 2 T. unbleached flour
> 1 1/2 c. light cream
> salt and pepper
> 1 c. brown rice cooked to 3 c.

Combine drained beans, celery, carrot, whole onion, bay leaf and parsley in a 3-quart saucepan with water. With lid on, bring to boil, then reduce and simmer gently about 3 hours or until beans are tender but not mushy. Add more water as needed during cooking. When beans are tender, add corn and remove whole onion, bay leaf and parsley. Heat through only.

Meanwhile, melt butter in 1-quart saucepan, saute onion and green pepper until golden, about 5 minutes. Remove from heat, stir in flour then cream. Return to heat, cook gently stirring until thickened, 3-5 minutes. Drain corn and beans as necessary, combine with sauce. Add salt and pepper to taste. Serve over the warm cooked rice.

GO WITHS: A simple green salad dressed with a light vinaigrette followed by tart green apples and sharp Cheddar or Brie wedges.

Pilaf Pignoli

Rice casseroles called pilaf are a staple of Middle Eastern cooking. To be authentic, add raisins at the last few minutes of cooking. This type of casserole is most versatile, as ingredients can be easily added or subtracted. It's also a good choice for the camp stove.

> 5 T. butter, divided
> 1 c. brown rice
> 2 1/2 c. water
> 1/2 c. sesame seeds
> 1 c. pignoli (pine nuts)
> 2 cloves garlic, minced
> 1 large onion, coarsely chopped
> 1 stalk celery with leaves, sliced thin
> 1 large carrot, grated coarsely
> 2 c. fresh mushrooms, sliced
> 1 t. marjoram
> 2 t. chervil
> salt and pepper
> 3 T. fresh coriander leaves, minced
>   or Italian flat-leaf parsley, minced

Melt half the butter in 3-quart saucepan. Saute rice briefly. Add water, cover and bring to boil. Meanwhile, brown sesame seeds and pignoli in 2 t. butter and add to rice pan. When rice has boiled, lower heat to simmer. Add remaining butter to skillet the seeds were cooked in, saute vegetables until golden, about 5 minutes. Season with herbs, salt and pepper. Add this also to rice, continue to cook until all water is absorbed and rice is tender. Sprinkle generously with minced coriander leaves or parsley.

GO WITHS: Any cooked green vegetable, allowed to cool in a vinaigrette dressing. Add slices of fresh tomatoes seasoned with basil.

Ropa Vieja

The literal translation from the Spanish is "old clothes." Chick peas are a high quality protein, distinctive in flavor and with a firm texture. They combine expecially well with tomatoes and high seasoning. Additionally, they tend to be the most easily digested legumes.

    1 lb. chick peas, soaked 2 hours
    1 T. vegetable oil
    1 large onion, minced
    2 cloves garlic, finely minced
    2 c. tomato puree
    1 T. chili powder
    salt and pepper
    1/2 t. ground cumin
    2-3 T. minced fresh parsley

Cook chick peas in water to cover over moderately-high heat, covered, adding more water as necessary. They should be crisp-tender in 1 1/2 hours. Heat oil in wide-based 3-quart saucepan and saute onions and garlic about 5 minutes. Add tomato puree and seasonings. Simmer gently about 10 minutes to gather flavor. Serve sprinkled with parsley.

GO WITHS: Lightly steamed green vegetables, such as broccoli, asparagus, green beans, peas or a combination of these, dressed with lemon butter. Serve with crusty bread or home-made biscuits.

Hearty Salads

When the weather is hot and muggy, it's nice to put a dinner together without lighting a stove. All salads made without greens should be allowed to marinate in their dressings, with at least some of the ingredients added when still warm to better absorb the flavors. Blanching cabbage-family vegetables removes some of the gaseous quality. To make cucumbers more digestible, peel and seed, then sprinkle with salt. After 15 minutes, rinse clear and pat dry.

Four Vegetable Platter:
Spiced Beets, Peas Mayonnaise,
Corn and Cheese Pompoms, Green Beans Chili

SPICED BEETS

> 2 c. small beets
> 1 onion in thin rings
> 3 T. red wine vinegar
> 4 T. olive oil
> 6 whole cloves
> 6 whole allspice
> 1 t. whole mustard seed
> 1-inch stick cinnamon

Cook beets until tender in water to cover with lid. Drain and peel while still hot. Combine with remaining ingredients while still hot. If you use canned beets, heat them in their liquid, drain and combine while still warm with the other ingredients. Turn frequently to distribute flavor. Allow to gather flavor at least 4 hours before serving.

PEAS MAYONNAISE

2 c. cooked peas, cooled or frozen peas, thawed
   and drained
2 t. finely minced fresh mint or 1/2 t. dried mint
1/2-3/4 c. freshly-made mayonnaise
1 T. Dijon mustard

Combine all ingredients and allow to gather flavor 1 hour.

CORN AND CHEESE POMPOMS

8 ounces soft cream cheese
1 clove garlic, mashed to paste
2 T. grated onion
1 t. crushed sage
salt and white pepper
2 c. cooked corn

Combine all ingredients but corn in a mixing bowl. Make
about 2 dozen balls of cheese mixture, forming them with
hands dipped in cold water to keep cheese from sticking.
Drain corn well and pat dry on a towel. Roll each cheese
ball in corn until it is evenly covered. Serve chilled.

GREEN BEANS CHILI

1 c. cooked whole green beans
1 c. cooked whole yellow beans
1/2 c. chili sauce
2-3 T. red wine vinegar
1/4 c. grated Parmesan

Drain both beans and while still warm, combine with
chili sauce and vinegar. Sauce should be rather thin.
Allow to gather flavor about an hour, turning occasionally.
When ready to serve, sprinkle generously with Parmesan.

The platter should be arranged with each salad in a lettuce
leaf to keep the flavors of the different dressings separate.
GO WITHS: Add some whole wheat bread sticks or
crackers and end with a refreshing lime or lemon sherbet.

Greek Salad

One summer on a trip to Greece, after a hot and dusty trek through ancient ruins, I ate a salad along with a glass of magnificent spring water. Feta cheese and imported olives are available in supermarkets. Imported olives bought in bulk have much more flavor than the canned ones from California.

>   8 large tomatoes, cut in eighths
>   3 cucumbers, halved, seeded, sliced
>   1 large onion in thin rings
>   1 large green pepper in thin strips
>   1 lb. feta cheese in small dice
>   1 1/4 c. imported black olives, sliced

Dressing:

>   8 T. light olive oil
>   3 T. red wine vinegar
>   2 T. drained capers
>   2 T. minced fresh parsley
>   3 cloves garlic, mashed to paste
>   salt and pepper

Combine vegetables in large glass bowl (for beauty of presentation). Peel cucumbers only if they have been waxed. Combine dressing ingredients in small jar with secure lid, shake vigorously, pour over salad. Toss well and allow to gather flavor about an hour. Serve slightly chilled.

Greeks don't add lettuce to their salad because their climate is too hot to grow salad greens successfully, but we can add them if we choose.

GO WITHS: Crusty bread or crisp bread sticks are pleasant to serve with this salad.

Mohave Salad

A fruit salad named for the California desert. It makes a refreshing hot weather meal.

> 6 large leaves Romaine lettuce, washed, dried, sliced
> 6 large leaves Boston lettuce, washed, dried, sliced
> 3 c. tart apples, cubed
> 2 c. orange sections
> 1 c. grapefruit sections
> 1 c. avocado slices
> 1/2 lemon
> 2 stalks celery with leaves, minced
> 4 scallions, minced
> 1 1/2 c. Cheddar, cubed
> 3/4 c. slivered almonds
> 3/4 c. sour cream or plain yogurt

Combine greens and line large salad bowl or individual plates. Grapefruit, orange and avocado will have to be peeled, but the colorful skin of the apple is too attractive to throw away. Avocado slices must be rubbed with a cut lemon to prevent them from discoloring. Pile fruit on the greens, top with the Cheddar and almond slivers. Individual plates may be topped with generous scoops of yogurt or sour cream. If you use a large bowl, pass the yogurt or sour cream separately.

GO WITHS: Hot, freshly-made grain muffins or biscuits are particularly tasty with this. For dessert, squares of gingerbread with custard sauce or slices of butter-rich pound cake (see Appendix).

Spiced Cauliflower and Broccoli

1 quart water
3 c. cauliflower in flowerets
3 c. broccoli in flowerets
1 green pepper in thin strips
2 stalks celery with leaves, minced
3 scallions, minced
2 grated carrots
1 c. chopped roasted peanuts
1/2 c. sesame seed

Dressing:

2 cloves garlic, mashed to a paste
1/4 c. white champagne vinegar
1/2 c. olive oil
salt to taste
1/2 t. crushed dried red chili
2 T. minced fresh parsley
1 T. minced fresh basil
   or 1 t. dried basil

Bring water to a boil and drop in cauliflower and broccoli. Cover, bring to a boil again and drain immediately through a colander. Add to salad bowl with remaining vegetables, seeds and nuts. In a small jar with a secure lid, combine dressing ingredients. Shake vigorously and pour over salad. Toss well and allow to marinate 2-3 hours before serving.

GO WITHS: Pile the salad on a bed of lettuce. Add a plate of pita bread cut into quarters and filled with herbed cream cheese.

Stuffed Avocado

Avocados are a member of the pear family, as their shape might indicate. Watercress naturally compliments the creamy avocado and bland pear. Unfortunately, this is not a salad that stands well, so make it no more than an hour before serving.

> 6 avocados, halved and pitted
> 3 Anjou pears, halved and cored
> 1/2 lemon
> lettuce leaves
> 1 bunch watercress, stems removed, chopped
> 2 T. minced scallion
> 1/2 c. sesame seed
> 1/2 c. slivered toasted almonds

Dressing:
> 2 cloves garlic, mashed to paste
> 1 T. olive oil
> salt and pepper
> 2 T. orange juice
> 2 T. grapefruit juice

Rub cut sides of avocados and pears with lemon to prevent browning, leaving skins intact. Make dressing and add watercress, scallion and sesame seed. This mixture may be made several hours ahead of time, if desired.

Just before serving, fill cavities of avocado and pear with dressing mixture. Generously sprinkle with almonds. Line dinner plates with lettuce leaves, arrange 2 avocado halves and one pear half on each. Serve as soon as possible. Plates may be garnished with radish roses, orange sections or celery and carrot sticks.

GO WITHS: You'll need only crisp breadsticks or crackers as an accompaniment. My choice for dessert is ice cream with brandy or rum. For a festive touch, heat the liqueur in a soup ladle over a candle flame, tip to light and pour over the ice cream while flaming.

Stuffed Tomato

6 large tomatoes, each about 1 lb.
salt
1 c. cucumber, seeded, in small dice
1 c. minced scallion
1 c. chopped stuffed green and black olives
3/4 c. celery with leaves in small dice
3 T. minced fresh parsley
1 c. fresh mustard mayonnaise
whole lettuce leaves
6 whole imported black olives

Slice top off each tomato and scoop out center with spoon. Reserve pulp for another use. Sprinkle insides with salt, turn upside down and allow to drain about 20 minutes. Rinse and wipe out each tomato very thoroughly. Do not peel since the skin will make a firmer wall to hold filling as well as providing more nutrition.

Sprinkle diced cucumber with salt and allow to drain in a sieve or colander, rinsing well after 20 minutes. Pat dry on a towel.

Combine cucumbers with scallion, celery, olives, and parsley. Add just enough mayonnaise to bind.

Line salad plates with lettuce leaves, place a tomato on each, fill cavities with vegetable mixture. Center a black olive on top. Pass additional mayonnaise at table.

NOTE: Reserved tomato pulp may be simmered gently for 30-40 minutes with sauteed onion, herbs and seasoning to make tomato sauce. Puree in blender or food processor if desired. Pack in sterilized canning jars or freeze in plastic tubs.

GO WITHS: Garnish each plate with steamed green vegetables cooled in vinaigrette, such as broccoli spears, zucchini sticks or green beans. Hot biscuits or bread sticks are good with this salad. Since the garden tomato season coincides with the fresh peach season, marinate some peeled halves in honey and Amaretto liqueur and top with whipped cream or vanilla ice cream.

Pasta

Since spaghetti, eggroll and wonton wrappers are made from the same dough, the legend may be accurate that Marco Polo brought pasta from China in the thirteenth century. Italians have since substituted eggs, which are rare in China, for water, making a richer and smoother pastry. In Italian households on either side of the Atlantic, making the week's supply of pasta used to be a day-long chore involving the entire family, but with a simple, hand-cranked machine, a little over a pound of excellent pasta in any thickness or width can be made in under an hour, half that time with an electric one. Most of the recipes in this chapter call for fresh, home-made pasta because it not only tastes better but is much more nutritious than the packaged variety.

Basic Pasta Dough

1 lb. unbleached flour, about 4 c.
4 eggs
1-2 T. water or olive oil

Place flour in mixing bowl, make a well in the center and
add the eggs. Work to a paste with hands, adding water
or oil only as needed for dough to adhere. It must not
be sticky. Wrap in plastic and let rest at least 15 minutes.

WORKING BY HAND: Knead dough on lightly-floured
board by folding in half, pressing hard with heel of the
hand, continuing this motion until dough becomes satiny,
at least 10 minutes. Pasta dough is very stiff and knead-
ing it sufficiently takes strength. Cut into 8 pieces, keeping each in the plastic until ready to be used. Roll out
each piece on floured board, making dough as thin as
possible. Dust with flour or fine cornmeal and set aside
while rolling out other pieces. Fold each rolled out piece
into fourths or eighths, and, using the side of the hand as
a guide, slice with a very sharp knife as thick or thin as
desired. Unroll strands and allow to dry or cook immediately.

USING A MACHINE: Knead by placing one-eighth of
the dough through the rollers at their widest setting, continue this 5-6 times until it becomes satiny. Set aside each
kneaded piece as above, then put each piece through rollers until desired thinness has been reached. Run each strip
through either thick or thin cutting blade. Strands may
be cooked immediately or frozen in plastic bags or dried.

Fettucinie Alla Pesto

Fettucine is always cooked fresh. The pasta is not allowed to dry. It is rolled out very thin and cut fine. It lends itself perfectly to subtle sauces, such as the very simple Alfredo, which is nothing more than butter, heavy cream and freshly-grated Parmesan. The central ingredient of a Pesto is basil, an annual herb that can be grown indoors on a very sunny windowsill during the winter when it would be otherwise unavailable. Dried basil cannot be substituted.

- 2 c. fresh basil leaves, stems removed
- 1 c. pignoli
- 3 cloves garlic
- 1/2 c. scallions in 1-inch slices
- 1/2-3/4 c. olive oil
- salt and pepper
- 3/4 c. freshly-grated Parmesan
- 1 1/2 lb. fettucine (pasta rolled out on setting No. 6-7, cut fine)

Using either a food processor or a blender, combine basil leaves, pignoli, garlic and scallions. Blend until thick and smooth. After the count of 10, slowly pour in oil, as for mayonnaise. By hand, fold in Parmesan, seasoning to taste. Turn sauce into small saucepan, heat very gently.

Boil about 3 quarts water; when bubbling rapidly, add fresh fettucine. Stir to keep strands from sticking together. Allow to cook only about 30 seconds, drain immediately into a colander, run under hot water to remove any excess flour. Turn into warm serving bowl, toss with Pesto and serve. Additional Parmesan may be passed at table.

NOTE: Since pignoli are hard to find and expensive, you may wish to substitute a third cup of basil leaves.

Sauce may be frozen for winter in small containers, but omit the cheese. Add sauce and freshly-grated cheese.

GO WITHS: Steamed broccoli or asparagus cooled in a vinaigrette, sprinkled with grated hard-boiled eggs (Mimosa). Fresh fruit in a pastry tart makes an elegant dessert.

Linguine Romano

Linguine is fine, flat spaghetti, just about the same size as fettucine.

> 3/4 c. butter, divided
> 3 scallions, minced
> 1 c. freshly-grated Parmesan
> 6 ounces cream cheese
> 1 t. dried basil
> salt and white pepper
> 2/3 c. dry white wine
> 1 lb. linguine
> 1/4 c. finely-minced onion
> 2 cloves minced garlic
> 3 T. minced fresh parsley

Melt 1/4 c. butter in small saucepan over moderate heat. Saute scallion about 1 minute. Add both cheeses and allow them to melt. Add basil and seasoning. Gradually add wine, keeping heat very low so sauce won't curdle. Keep warm.

Cook linguine in rapidly boiling water until it is barely tender, about 2 minutes. Drain immediately in colander.

In a large skillet, melt remaining butter and saute onion and garlic quickly. Remove from heat, toss with linguine thoroughly, return to burner and heat through only. Remove from burner, add sauce and toss well. Serve from skillet, sprinkled generously with parsley.

GO WITHS: Coleslaw with slivers of green pepper, shredded carrot and fennel. Use as little mayonnaise as possible. End with a dish of fresh pineapple marinated in rum.

Pasta Giobbi

Named for a cookbook author and restauranteur, this is based on a Southern Italian peasant dish. Use fresh tomatoes when they are in season. Otherwise, use canned tomatoes, drained.

    1 1/2 lb. fresh spinach, washed and chopped
    1/4 c. minced fresh parsley
    1 lb. Ricotta or small curd cottage cheese
    3 eggs
    3/4 c. Parmesan

Sauce:

    1-2 t. olive oil
    2 cloves garlic, finely minced
    1/2 c. chopped onion
    3 c. tomatoes, peeled, chopped
    1 t. basil
    1/2 t. oregano
    salt and pepper
    1 c. red wine

    1 1/2 c. diced small zucchini
    1 lb. noodles, rolled on setting No. 4, cut in
      2-inch lengths

Lightly oil a large skillet and steam spinach in its own moisture, tightly covered, about 2 minutes. Remove immediately to a colander and squeeze out any remaining moisture. Combine with parsley, Ricotta, eggs and Parmesan. Set aside.

Make sauce in a 2-quart saucepan heating olive oil and sauteing garlic and onion until golden, about 2 minutes. Add tomatoes, herbs and seasoning. Simmer together 20 minutes. Add wine and simmer another 20 minutes. Meanwhile, boil 3 quarts water, cook pasta until barely tender, about 3 minutes. Drain immediately and rinse to remove excess starch.

In a large oven-proof casserole, combine spinach mixture, drained pasta, tomato sauce and zucchini dice. Bake in preheated 350 degree oven 20-30 minutes. Pass additional freshly-grated Parmesan at table.

GO WITHS: Serve hot, crusty bread and a crisp green salad. Have a dessert of tart apples or slightly under-ripe pears with a rich cheese such as Brie or Camembert.

Frank and Jane's Macaroni

Cooked for me many years ago by a young man who lived with our family a while, it remains a favorite quick dinner.

> 1 lb. macaroni or home-made noodles, rolled on
>   setting No. 4, cut thick and into 2-inch lengths,
>   fresh or dried
> 1/4 c. butter
> 3/4 c. chopped onion
> 1/3 c. green pepper in small dice
> 1 c. sliced fresh mushrooms
> 3 c. grated sharp Cheddar
> 1 T. Dijon mustard
> salt and pepper to taste

Cook noodles or macaroni in rapidly boiling water until just barely tender and drain immediately in colander.

Melt butter in 3-quart saucepan, saute onion, green pepper and mushrooms until tender, about 5 minutes. Add drained cooked pasta and cheese, stirring to melt and combine well. If too dry, add more butter. Stir in mustard and seasonings.

GO WITHS: A stir-fry of scallions, green pepper slivers and bean sprouts, seasoned with grated fresh ginger-root, garlic and soy sauce. For dessert, pear or peach halves briefly cooked with whole allspice and nutmeg in white wine instead of water and served warm.

Soufflé Noodle Ring

Filled rings of pastry, rice or noodles are a particularly good choice for a buffet.

    2 c. noodles, rolled on setting No. 6, cut wide
        and in 2-inch lengths
    4 eggs, separated
    1 1/4 c. grated Cheddar
    1 t. Dijon mustard
    salt and white pepper
    1 additional egg white
    1/2 c. dry bread crumbs

Filling:
    2 c. steamed asparagus in 2-inch lengths
        or small broccoli flowerets
    3 T. butter
    1/2 c. minced onion
    3/4 c. sliced fresh mushrooms
    salt and pepper
    1 t. marjoram
    3 T. unbleached flour
    1/4 c. dry sherry
    1 c. light cream, scalded

Cook noodles in rapidly boiling water until just tender, if fresh only 30 seconds, if dry about 3 minutes. Drain and rinse in cold water. Meanwhile, beat yolks with cheese, mustard and seasoning. Whip whites only until they reach soft peak stage. Combine yolk mixture with drained noodles, then fold in whites gently but thoroughly. Pour into well-greased 2-quart ring mold dusted with bread crumbs. Bake in preheated 350 degree oven half an hour. Turn out immediately onto warm platter, arrange filling in middle.

While souffle is baking, steam asparagus or broccoli and set aside. Melt butter in 9-10 inch skillet and saute onion until transparent, then add mushrooms and seasonings. Saute another 3-4 minutes. Remove from heat, stir in flour, then liquids. Return to heat, simmer and stir until quite thick. Add asparagus pieces or broccoli flowerets and heat through. Keep warm until ring is ready to be filled.

GO WITHS: When served as the hot dish of a summer buffet, a colorful accompaniment is the Four Vegetable Platter (see page 45) and small stuffed tomatoes. Add some breadsticks, end with thin wedges of honeydew, cantelope and watermelon. For a simple dinner, serve with the stuffed tomatoes alone and one of the melons.

Pastries

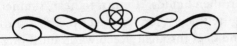

Light, flaky pastry is one of the most delectable and versatile foods. Generally I recommend unbleached flour for lightness. There are some pastries in this section that are heartier and work well with whole wheat, as I indicate. All these pastries can be made in bite-size for party snacks.

Aloo Samosa

A favorite hors d'oeurvre in India, it can also be a satisfying main dish.

Filling:
> 1/4 c. butter
> 1 1/2 c. onion, peeled, minced
> 1 large clove garlic, minced
> 1/4 t. minced fresh ginger root
> 1 t. cumin seed
> 1/2 t. mustard seed
> 2 c. unpeeled potato, diced
> 1 1/2 t. curry powder
> 1 t. turmeric
> 1 t. ground coriander
> salt to taste
> 3-inch length lemon peel

Pastry:

> 3 c. whole wheat flour
> 6 T. melted butter
> few drops water
> vegetable oil for deep frying

Melt butter in 2-quart saucepan and fry half the onion, the ginger, garlic, cumin and mustard seeds until golden brown, about 15 minutes. Add potatoes, stir and fry about 3 minutes. Add remaining spices, lemon peel, and 1/4 c. water. Simmer, covered, until potatoes are nearly tender, about 10 minutes. Add remaining onion, continue to simmer, adding water as necessary until all is tender. Cool before filling pastry.

Make a well in the flour in a mixing bowl, pour in melted butter. Stir with hands to make a firm dough, adding drops of water as needed for it to adhere. Knead well on lightly-floured board about 10 minutes for dough to become smooth and elastic. Wrap in plastic or towel, allow to rest 15 minutes. Divide dough into 18 balls, keeping them covered. Roll out each ball to a flat 6-inch round, place a spoonful of filling in middle, fold three sides over to form a completely enclosed triangle. Seal all seams with water.

Heat oil in 2-quart saucepan to the depth of 1 1/2 inches. When a cube of bread browns in 30 seconds, oil is sufficiently hot for frying. If you have a deep-fry thermometer, the temperature should be 375 degrees. Add one or two samosas at a time, fry until browned and crisp, turning once. Drain on toweling, keep warm until all are fried. Serve hot.

GO WITHS: Serve with fresh spinach steamed less than one minute in a big covered skillet with Chinese sesame oil, sesame seeds and soy sauce. Fresh fruit or ice cream makes a refreshing dessert.

Pâté Pantin

A version of a classic French Pate en Croute. Baking individual squares makes serving easy, particularly on a buffet. It may be served room temperature and travels well for picnics.

Pastry:

> 2/3 c. butter
> 2 1/2 c. unbleached flour
> 1 egg
> 1/4 c. dry white wine
> beaten egg for glaze

Filling:

> 5 c. chopped onion
> 3 cloves garlic, mashed
> 2 T. butter
> 1 lb. sliced fresh mushrooms
> 1 1/2 c. toasted slivered almonds
> 2 T. minced fresh parsley
> 2 t. tarragon
> 2 t. chervil
> 1 t. Dijon mustard
> 1/2 c. tomato paste
> 3/4 c. cooked brown rice

Make pastry by working butter into flour with 2 table knives until it is evenly distributed. Combine egg and wine, add to bowl and stir in well with one of the knives. Mix only until dough adheres to itself, do not overwork or pastry will be tough. Wrap in plastic and chill 30 minutes to 1 hour. Pastry will keep in the refrigerator for several days or it may be frozen.

While pastry is chilling, prepare filling. In a large, heavy skillet, saute onion and garlic in butter until golden, about

3 minutes. Add mushrooms, cook and stir another few minutes until tender. Add remaining ingredients. Simmer over low heat about 10 minutes for flavors to blend. Taste for seasoning and cool to room temperature before filling pastry.

Divide pastry into 6 portions, roll out each on a lightly-floured board into an 8-inch square, making the pastry quite thin. Heap some filling in the middle, cut off corners so pastry will not have extra thick areas. Fold over like an envelope to encase filling, sealing seams with water. Place pastry squares on baking sheet, brush with egg glaze and bake in preheated 425 degree oven about 25 minutes or until golden brown.

GO WITHS: A steamed green vegetable such as fresh broccoli sprinkled with lemon juice. Marinated oranges are a good winter fresh fruit dessert. Peel oranges, slice thickly and marinate in a little orange liqueur (Cointreau, Grand Marnier, Cusinier Orange or Triple Sec) 2-3 hours or even overnight. Garnish with fine shreds of orange zest (the skin without the white pith).

Heaped Pizza

Many years ago, friends took us to their favorite Italian restaurant in Washington, D.C. where we were served a pizza with a separately-sauteed vegetable topping. While I never had a pizza resembling it in all of Italy, the interesting texture makes it worth the effort.

Pastry:

    1 T. active dry yeast
    1 1/3 c. warm water
    3 c. whole wheat flour
    1 c. unbleached flour
    1/2 c. soy flour
    1 T. olive oil

Topping:

    3 T. olive oil
    3 c. thin onion rings
    2 large green peppers in thin strips
    1 lb. sliced fresh mushrooms
    1 c. thinly-sliced fennel or celery
    3 T. minced fresh parsley
    1 c. sliced black olives

Filling:

    3 c. tomato sauce (see Appendix)
    1 1/2 lb. sliced Mozzarella

    freshly-grated Parmesan
    red pepper flakes

Dissolve yeast in warm water, allow to rest a few minutes. Put flours in mixing bowl, combine thoroughly with oil and yeasted water. Knead vigorously on lightly-floured board for about 10 minutes, until dough is smooth and elastic. Place in cloth-covered bowl in a warm, draft free spot to rise about 2 hours. It can also rise more slowly overnight in the refrigerator, allowing about 12 hours. When ready, knead again several times. Divide in half and roll out each piece to fit a 12-inch round pan or place on a baking sheet. Spread generously with tomato sauce and Mozzarella slices. Preheat oven to 400 degrees and bake 15 minutes or until crust has browned and cheese is bubbling. Pie may be allowed to cool, then wrapped in plastic and frozen, if desired.

While pizza is baking, heat olive oil in large skillet and saute all vegetables until crisp-tender, about 6 minutes. If necessary, add a drop or two more oil to prevent sticking and burning. Cook over moderately high heat. Stir in parsley and olives just to heat through. When pie is removed from oven, distribute vegetables on top. Cut in wedges and serve, passing Parmesan and pepper flakes at table.

GO WITHS: Crisp salad of mixed greens dressed with a strong mustard vinaigrette (see Appendix).

Quiche

Quiche (the French word for custard tart) is traditionally served as an appetizer. Cut in very small wedges, it makes an elegant cocktail snack. It's also a fine lunch or supper main dish.

Pastry:

>   1 1/4 c. unbleached flour
>   4 T. unsalted butter
>   2 T. vegetable shortening
>   3 T. cold water
>   egg white for glazing

Basic Filling:

>   4 eggs
>   1 1/2 c. scalded light cream
>   salt and white pepper
>   dash nutmeg
>   3 T. minced scallion
>   3/4 c. grated Swiss
>   3/4 c. grated Cheddar
>   3 T. minced fresh parsley

Make pastry by cutting fats into flour in mixing bowl with 2 table knives until well mixed. Add water, stir in with one knife until dough holds together. Do not over-work or it will become tough. Wrap in plastic and chill 1 hour. Pastry may be kept in the refrigerator at this point several days or frozen.

Divide chilled dough in half, roll out on a lightly-floured board quite thin. Fit each rolled half into an 8-inch pie or flan tin. Brush bottoms with egg white and chill again at least 10 minutes. At this point also, pastry may be wrapped in plastic and kept several days, refrig-erated, or frozen.

In a mixing bowl, beat eggs with whisk, gradually beat in cream and seasonings, except parsley. Divide scallions among bottoms of 2 pans, then the two cheeses. Pour in the custard, top with parsley and bake in preheated 400 degree oven 30 minutes or until pastry edges are beginning to brown and custard is set. Allow to rest 5-10 minutes before cutting. Quiche should always be served lukewarm, never hot, this will prevent "watering."

Variations:

1. 8-10 partially-steamed thin spears of broccoli or asparagus, arranged in a spoke pattern on top of unbaked custard. Spaces between spears may be filled with small wedges of seeded tomato.

2. 1 c. sliced fresh mushrooms, blanched 30 seconds in boiling water and patted dry, distributed on top of unbaked custard with 1 t. marjoram.

3. 1/2 c. tomato puree beaten into eggs with only 1 c. scalded cream and 1 t. Dijon mustard. Sprinkle with parsley and 1 t. basil.

GO WITHS: In warm weather fresh fruit on lettuce leaves, dressed with sour cream and chives. In colder weather, stir-fry green pepper slivers, sliced water chestnuts, shredded Chinese cabbage, bean sprouts and grated carrot 2-3 minutes in a little vegetable oil, toss with sesame seeds and soy sauce as it is served. Fruit sherbet would be my choice for dessert.

Vol-Au-Vent Provençal

Large puff pastry cases, or pie shells, have been important in French cooking for centuries, appearing as early as 1350. The pastry in this recipe is an English version used in Cornish Pasty as well as Steak and Kidney Pie. It sounds complicated but is surer and easier to prepare than traditional French puff pastry and reduces the amount of butter by substituting some vegetable shortening. Since the pastry shell, vegetable filling and sauce are each made separately, this is an ideal make-ahead dish. If desired, cases and sauce can be made in quantity and frozen.

Pastry:

2 c. unbleached flour
3 oz. cold butter
1/3 c. ice water
3 oz. cold vegetable shortening

Filling:

1 T. olive oil
1 c. eggplant in quartered slices, unpeeled
1 c. small zucchini, sliced, unpeeled
1/2 c. small mushroom caps
1/2 c. blanched broccoli flowerets
1/2 c. freshly-grated Parmesan
1/2 c. fresh, soft bread crumbs

Sauce:

1 oz. butter
2 T. finely-minced onion
1 T. finely-minced celery leaves
3 T. flour
1 c. light cream
1/2 c. tomato puree
salt and pepper
1/2 t. basil

Make pastry by placing flour in mixing bowl. Cut half the butter in with two table knives or pastry blender. Add water, combining with one of the knives, adding more water if necessary. Turn out onto lightly-floured board and knead 2-3 times with the heel of the hand to distribute butter. Roll out dough to an 18-inch oblong, dot upper two-thirds with half the shortening. Fold plain part of pastry over half the dotted part, then fold remaining dotted section over all. Turn so open ends of pastry are facing you, ridge ends with the rolling pin to seal in fat, then ridge down length of pastry. Roll out pastry to original 18-inch shape. Dot in the same fashion with remaining butter, fold over as before, turn and seal ends. Roll out a third time, dot with remaining shortening and fold as before. Wrap in plastic and chill at least 1 hour. Work quickly, rolling the pastry so that fats do not melt as you combine them. If it is warm, it may be necessary to chill pastry between "turns." Pastry may be frozen at this stage.

Roll out chilled pastry to fit a 2-inch deep 10-inch pie or flan tin. Make a simple rolled edge round the top without crimping, chill 10 minutes. Line case with wax paper and fill with rice, dry beans or metal pie weights. Bake in preheated 425 degree oven about 15 minutes, until edges begin to brown. Remove weights and paper, bake another 10 minutes for bottom to brown. Shell may be frozen before and after it is baked, if desired.

While pastry is chilling the first time, make sauce by melting butter in small saucepan. Saute onion and celery leaves 3-4 minutes, remove from heat and stir in flour, then cream and tomato puree. Season and return to gentle heat to simmer, stirring, until thickened. Sauce may be frozen if preferred or kept warm with wax paper pressed directly on its surface to absorb the skin which will cause lumps.

Prepare the filling by heating a little vegetable oil in a skillet, saute eggplant until tender. Remove and keep warm. Wipe out skillet, heat a little more oil and saute zucchini in the same manner. Remove to another bowl and keep warm. Clean out skillet again, then melt a little butter and saute mushrooms 2-3 minutes.

ASSEMBLY: Pour warm sauce over bottom of warm baked shell, then arrange eggplant with skin upmost in a ring around outer edge. Form a ring inside that with the zucchini, then with the mushrooms. Fill center with broccoli. Dot all over very lightly with butter. Combine soft crumbs and Parmesan, sprinkle over vegetables and heat through in 350 degree oven about 15 minutes. Finished pie may be frozen as well, thawing completely before reheating.

GO WITHS: For a winter buffet add a mixed green salad with red onion rings in a mustard vinaigrette. A more formal dinner or buffet could include a first course of Linguine Romano (see page 55) and the colorful Four Vegetable Platter (see page 45). A handsome dessert for either occasion is Imperial Rice (see Appendix).

Spanakopita

The Middle East has a pastry called phyllo used for savory pies and rich desserts. It is usually available in supermarket freezer sections.

    10 sheets phyllo pastry, 14 x 11-inch
    1/2 c. melted butter
    1 1/4 lb. fresh spinach, washed, shredded
    salt and pepper
    2 c. cottage cheese, well-drained
    3/4 c. minced onion
    1 c. Feta cheese, crumbled
    3 whole eggs
    1 t. thyme
    1/2 t. ginger

Lightly grease an 11 x 7-inch baking dish. Lay a sheet of pastry in the pan and brush lightly with butter. It should hang over the sides of the pan all round. Continue with four more sheets, brushing with butter also.

Meanwhile, place spinach in a colander and sprinkle with 2 T. salt. Allow to drain about 20 minutes, then rinse thoroughly and squeeze quite dry. Combine spinach with drained cottage cheese, feta and onion. Beat eggs with thyme, ginger and pepper, add to spinach mixture. Taste for seasoning. Pour filling into pastry-lined pan. Fold over pastry all round. Lay remaining sheets of pastry on top, brushing each with butter as well and seal edges with water. Make a few steam slits in top, bake in preheated 350 degree oven 30-40 minutes. Remove and allow to rest at least 5 minutes before cutting into squares. Serve lukewarm or room temperature.

GO WITHS: Thinly-sliced fresh tomatoes layered with slices of cucumber and onion rings, simply dressed in olive oil. If the tomato season is past try grilled tomato halves or a tomato stew seasoned with oregano and lemon juice. For dessert marinate fresh, sliced fruit in a little rum, passing whipped cream, if desired.

Soup / Stew

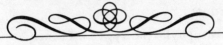

African Peanut Soup

Much of East African cooking uses a hot curry deriving from the Indian subcontinent's colonizers throughout the Third World. It is often bound with a peanut sauce similar to the Southeast Asian style. I've reduced the quantity of chilies for American taste, but you can easily add more.

- 8 oz. natural peanut butter
- 3 T. tomato paste
- 1 c. cold water
- 4 large tomatoes, peeled, chopped
- 2 large onions, peeled, minced
- 2 large fresh green chilies, minced
    or 1 1/2 t. dried red pepper flakes
- 3 cloves garlic, minced fine
- 2 stalks celery with leaves, minced
- 2 t. salt
- 1 t. ground cumin
- 1 c. light cream or half and half

Combine peanut butter, tomato paste and water in small saucepan and simmer gently 15 minutes. Set aside. In a 2 1/2-quart saucepan combine all remaining ingredients but cream and simmer gently 30 minutes. Then add peanut mixture to vegetables as well as cream and heat through, do not allow it to boil or cream will curdle. Taste for seasoning and serve very hot.

GO WITHS: Indian flat bread, such as Poori or Chappati, or the more available pita pocket bread. A salad of shredded cabbage mixed with slivers of green pepper and carrot and dressed with soy sauce, ginger and Chinese sesame oil. Finish with fresh fruit.

Chunky Vichysoisse

One of the very few truly successful cold soups, it is an American version of the French Potage Parmentier. The original recipe calls for a good deal of chicken broth, as do all French creamed soups, but the addition of egg yolks compensates nicely.

2 c. potatoes, cubed, boiled with skin
1 clove garlic
1 1/2 c. milk
1 c. heavy cream
salt and white pepper
2 egg yolks
1 t. Dijon-style mustard
3 T. dry sherry
1/2 c. minced scallion including green tops
2 T. minced fresh parsley

Drain boiled potatoes well, remove skins if desired. Place half the potatoes in blender or food processor with garlic and enough milk to make a smooth loose paste. Remove to mixing bowl, stir in remaining potatoes, milk and cream. Add seasoning, mustard, beaten yolks, sherry and scallion. Combine well, adding more cream if soup is too thick. Chill for at least 2 hours. Serve in chilled soup bowls sprinkled with parsley.

In cool weather, this soup may be served hot. Turn completed mixture from mixing bowl into 2-quart saucepan and heat gently, being sure it never comes to a boil or it will curdle.

GO WITHS: When the soup is served cold, accompany with bread sticks and a salad of sliced tomatoes and cucumbers. In cooler weather, serve it hot with fresh, hot biscuits and lightly blanched broccoli spears and carrot sticks steeped in a vinaigrette sauce.

Minestrone

There are as many variations of this soup as villages in Italy. This version is based on the Calabrian style, a province in the toe of the Boot. A pressure cooker will reduce the long cooking required or a crock-pot can be left to simmer unattended for the day.

1/4 c. chick peas, soaked overnight
1/4 c. pinto beans, soaked overnight
1/4 c. pea beans, soaked overnight
3 large chopped onions
1 c. chopped fennel or celery stalks
2 large carrots, scraped and sliced
2 T. miso paste (soy bean paste)
1/4 c. barley
1/4 c. brown lentils
1/4 c. yellow or green dried peas
1 lb. 12 oz. can plum tomatoes
1 1/2 t. basil
1 t. oregano
1 T. Dijon mustard
salt and red pepper flakes
3 bay leaves
1 1/2 c. freshly-grated Parmesan

Drain beans that have soaked overnight, combine them in a large, 3-4 quart saucepan with half the onion and half the fennel or celery, half the carrots, the miso and 2 quarts water. Cover and simmer gently for 2 hours. Add remaining ingredients except Parmesan, cover and continue to simmer until all beans are tender, at least another hour, perhaps two. If soup becomes too thick, add some tomato juice. Taste for seasoning. Serve very hot, with a generous topping of Parmesan on each bowl.

GO WITHS: Crusty, hot garlic bread followed by a green salad made of at least half spinach leaves or pungent sorrel or arugula, thin onion rings and sliced raw mushrooms. Dress with lemon juice, a dash of olive oil and dust well with sieved eggs. For dessert make a hot fruit compote with quickly simmered halved peaches, pears, pineapple chunks and banana slices in red wine spiced with a cinnamon stick and 4-5 whole allspice. Pass whipped cream or vanilla ice cream at table.

Hot and Sour Tofu Pot

A classic Chinese soup from Szechwan Province which specializes in hot and spicy dishes. Three different soy bean products are used here: tofu or bean curd, cellophane noodles or bean thread and miso paste making this a high protein dish. The stock can be made in quantity and stored in the freezer indefinitely.

Vegetable Stock:

>   1 whole carrot
>   2 stalks celery with leaves
>   1 peeled onion
>   2 bay leaves
>   2 T. miso paste
>   6 peppercorns
>   7 c. water

>   1 lb. tofu (bean curd), drained
>   4 T. soy sauce, divided
>   1 T. Chinese sesame oil
>   1 T. dry sherry
>   2 c. cellophane noodles (bean thread), soaked
>   in warm water
>   4 dried black mushrooms, soaked and minced
>   1 c. sliced fresh mushrooms
>   4 T. cider vinegar
>   1/2 t. Szechwan peppercorns
>   or 1/4 t. Tabasco or chili oil
>   1/2 c. bamboo shoots, sliced
>   1 bunch scallions in 1-inch pieces
>   3 c. shredded Chinese cabbage

Make stock by combining all ingredients in 2 1/2 quart saucepan and simmering together about 40 minutes. Strain before using. Store in covered jar in the refrigerator for several days or freeze in plastic tubs. Poured into hot, sterilized jars, it may be kept on the shelf.

Cut drained tofu into thin julienne strips, toss with 2 T. soy sauce, sesame oil and sherry. Allow to marinate at least 15 minutes. Soak bean thread. In a 3-4 quart saucepan, bring stock to boil, lower to simmer and add both mushrooms and soaking liquid, vinegar, peppercorns, and remaining soy sauce. Cook together 5 minutes, drain noodles and add. When stew is quite hot, about 2 minutes, add tofu with marinade and remaining ingredients. Stir together over moderate heat until steaming, 1-2 minutes. Serve quickly so vegetables retain crispness. At table, pass chili oil, if desired.

GO WITHS: Bread sticks or crackers followed by an Armenian Salad, made by combining a strong mustard vinaigrette with diced, peeled cucumber, sliced radishes, celery in small dice, sliced black olives and coarsely-chopped walnuts. Toss and let gather flavor while making the soup. Serve on shredded Romaine lettuce or Chinese cabbage.

Dahl-Chana

2 c. red or brown lentils
6 c. water
2 large carrots, sliced
1 large onion, peeled, sliced
1 1/2 c. chick peas, soaked 2 hours at least
3 cloves garlic, chopped
1 t. minced ginger root
2 t. turmeric
2 t. cumin seed
1 small fresh chili, minced fine
   or 1/2 t. cayenne
2 t. ground coriander
1 T. curry powder
2 c. tomatoes, peeled, coarsely chopped
2 medium onions, sliced

In a large 3-4 quart saucepan, combine lentils, water, carrots, large sliced onion and garlic. Bring to boil, covered, reduce heat and simmer gently about 1 1/2 hours. Lentils should be very tender. With a little vigorous stirring, they will puree lightly.

Meanwhile, drain soaking chick peas, place in a 2 1/2 quart saucepan with water to cover. Cover pan with lid and bring to boil, then reduce heat and simmer, covered, 2-3 hours, or until tender but still firm. When cooked, drain off any remaining liquid and combine with lentil puree as well as remaining ingredients. You will need a 3-4 quart saucepan for this stage of the stew. Simmer together at least 30 minutes. Taste for seasoning, thin with water or tomato juice if necessary. Serve very hot, garnished with coriander leaves or flat-leaf parsley.

GO WITHS: Traditional curry accompaniments of Indian flat bread or pita and a selection of condiments such as chutney, pickled lemons in mustard, peppered cauliflower, orange sections, freshly-grated coconut, chopped cashews or peanuts, and cooling diced cucumber in yogurt. For dessert, fresh fruit.

Pasta Stew

A basic peasant dish throughout southern Italy and Sicily. There seldom is meat in this stew, since most poor Europeans have meat only on holidays.

       2 T. olive oil
       2 medium carrots, sliced thin
       2 large onions, chopped
       2 cloves garlic, minced fine
       1 c. fresh parsley, minced
       2 t. basil
          or 3 T. fresh basil, minced
       salt and pepper
       4 large tomatoes, peeled and chopped
       1/2 c. red wine
       2 small zucchini, sliced
       1/2 lb. whole wheat macaroni
          or home-made fresh noodles in 2-inch lengths
       1/2 c. butter
       1 c. pignoli (pine nuts)
       3/4 c. freshly-grated Parmesan

Heat oil in a wide-bottomed 2 1/2-3 quart saucepan and saute carrots, onions and garlic until tender, about 8 minutes. Add herbs, tomatoes, wine, zucchini and seasoning. Simmer over low heat about 20 minutes.

Bring several quarts of water to the boil and cook pasta until barely tender, drain under cold water immediately. Melt butter in 10-inch skillet, lightly saute pignoli, add drained pasta and stir to coat. Add buttered noodles and pignoli to stew pan. Cook together about 5 minutes to combine flavors and serve very hot. Pass more Parmesan at table.

GO WITHS: Crusty bread or bread sticks and a salad of grated raw turnip and carrots with sliced green scallions in freshly-made mustard mayonnaise and a few capers. For dessert an Italian classic, Zabaglione (see Appendix).

Stuffed Vegetables

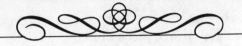

Bermuda Onion

6 large, mild Bermuda onions, each weighing
   about 1 lb., peeled
1/4 c. soft butter
3/4 c. dry whole wheat bread crumbs
salt and pepper
1 t. crumbled sage leaves
1 c. grated sharp Cheddar
1 t. Dijon-style mustard
2/3 c. finely-chopped roasted peanuts

Bring several quarts of water to boil in large saucepan or
stockpot. Cook onions at rolling boil 10 minutes with
lid, then drain well. Using a small sharp knife, scoop out
inner onion leaving a shell of 2-3 layers. Mince removed
onion and combine in a mixing bowl with remaining ingredients. Stuff onion shells with mixture and place in
buttered shallow baking pan, topping each onion with a
large pat of butter. Bake in preheated 350 degree oven
30 minutes. Serve very hot.

GO WITHS: Freshly-made green noodles tossed in garlic
butter with freshly-grated Parmesan cheese. Add a salad
of sliced baby zucchini and tomatoes marinated in vinaigrette 1 hour.

Acorn Squash

One of a thousand varieties of squash, most of which
originated in the Andes.

> 3 medium-large squash, halved crosswise
>   and seeded
> 1/4 c. soft butter
> salt and pepper
> 1 t. thyme
> 1 t. marjoram
> 1 1/2 c. coarsely-chopped walnuts
> 1 c. fresh sliced mushrooms
> 1 T. minced fresh parsley

Acorns should be cut so that the halves will have a
scalloped edge. To steady them so they will remain up-
right, remove a thin slice from the bottom. Boil several
quarts of water in a very large saucepan or stockpot, cook
halves, covered, 10 minutes. Remove and drain well.
Meanwhile, combine remaining ingredients in a mixing
bowl and divide among the par-boiled squash. Dish may
be prepared to this point several hours ahead or the day
before. Place in shallow baking pan with 1/2-inch hot
water and bake in preheated 350 degree oven 25 minutes
or until tender. Brush squash edges with butter before
serving.

GO WITHS: For a simple supper, green pepper quarters,
sauteed in butter with sliced onion, garlic, salt and pepper.
It holds well so can be included on a buffet with the
acorns. Add a bowl of cole slaw seasoned with Roque-
fort cheese and black olives. Cheesecake with a glazed
fruit topping also stands well and usually feeds a large
group.

Artichoke

First eaten in Italy around 1400, artichokes quickly
spread to the rest of Europe and England. However, a
small coastal region of California near Monterey Bay is
considered the artichoke capital of the world. European
varieties tend to be much smaller and are usually eaten
whole because the furry choke is undeveloped.

> 6 very large artichokes, stemmed and points
>   trimmed
> 1 lemon, halved
> 1/2 c. butter
> 1/2 c. celery in small dice
> 1 c. minced onion
> 2 cloves garlic, minced fine
> salt and pepper
> 1 T. minced fresh parsley
> 2 t. marjoram
> 1 1/2 c. sliced fresh mushrooms
> 1 c. wheat germ
> 1 1/2 c. dry white wine
>
> Butter Sauce:
>
> 1 c. melted butter
> salt and white pepper
> 1 T. lemon juice

Rub cut edges and bottoms of artichokes with lemon to
prevent discoloring. Working from the center, spread
leaves apart until you have come to the choke or furry
center. Spoon it out and discard, sprinkling the area with
lemon. Place prepared artichokes in shallow baking dish.
To maintain color, do not use aluminum or tin-lined
copper.

Melt butter in 9-10 inch skillet and gently saute onion,
celery, garlic, herbs and seasoning. After 3 minutes, add
mushrooms and cook another 3 minutes. Remove from

heat, stir in wheat germ to form a paste that barely holds
shape. Add more wheat germ if necessary. Divide filling
into sixths, spoon into central cavity and between leaves
of each artichoke. Pour in wine and 1 c. water. Bake in
preheated 350 degree oven 45 minutes. Serve warm or
chilled, spooning cooking liquid over each serving. Pass
    Melt butter; add pepper and lemon juice. Pass sauce at
table for dipping the leaves.

GO WITHS: An attractive summer buffet can be arranged
around stuffed artichokes by adding platters of cheese-
stuffed celery with olives and radish roses, cucumbers in
minted yogurt, stuffed eggs alternating with quartered tomatoes in olive oil. For dessert, continue the stuffed
theme with fruit compote in a hollowed out watermelon
shell.

Cabbage Mexicali

Filling:

> 1 1/2 c. pinto beans, soaked and cooked to 2 1/2 c.
> 2 T. vegetable oil
> 1 c. chopped onion
> 2 cloves garlic, minced
> 1 minced fresh green chili
>   or. 1/2 t. dried red pepper flakes

Sauce:

> 3 c. tomatoes, peeled and chopped
> 1 t. ground cumin
> 2 finely-minced green chilies
> salt

> 1 dozen large cabbage leaves, blanched

Drain cooked pinto beans, add them to heated oil in a large 12-inch skillet. Add remaining filling ingredients and saute over low heat until onions wilt and cook into beans. Add more oil as necessary to prevent sticking. Meanwhile, in a 2-quart saucepan, combine sauce ingredients and simmer gently about 15 minutes for flavors to combine. If sauce is too thick, thin with tomato juice and adjust seasoning.

Lay softened cabbage leaves flat on a table top, place a large spoonful of bean sauce in the middle of each leaf, roll up to enclose completely. Line a shallow baking dish with a little tomato sauce and arrange stuffed rolls inside. Cover with remaining sauce and heat through in preheated 350 degree oven about 20 minutes.

GO WITHS: Crusty bread and a traditional Spanish salad of sliced oranges and thinly-sliced onions arranged overlapping on individual plates. A dessert of freshly-made bunuelos, known as churros in Spain, Beignets in France and French doughnuts in this country. The batter is cream puff pastry (see page 68), deep-fried and dusted with powdered sugar.

Eggplant

3 medium-small eggplants, about 6-inches long,
   halved lengthwise
3 T. butter
1 c. chopped onion
1/4 c. minced celery
2 cloves garlic, mashed
1 c. sliced fresh mushrooms
1 1/2 c. tomatoes, peeled, chopped
salt and pepper
1 t. basil
1 t. oregano
1/2 t. dry mustard
1 1/2 c. pignoli (pine nuts)
   or toasted, slivered almonds
1/2 lb. Mozzarella, sliced

Bring several quarts of water to the boil in a large saucepan or stockpot, plunge in eggplant halves and cook, covered, for 6 minutes. Remove and drain well. Scoop out
interior, leaving a very thin shell. Melt butter, saute onion, celery and garlic in a 10-inch skillet until golden,
about 3 minutes. Add mushrooms and saute another 3
minutes. Add tomatoes, seasonings and chopped eggplant. Simmer gently together about 10 minutes, covered. Add toasted pignoli or almonds and divide filling
among the six shells. Cover each eggplant with Mozzarella slices and place in a lightly-buttered baking dish. Bake
in preheated 350 degree oven about 30 minutes. Cheese
should be bubbling and beginning to brown.

GO WITHS: Steamed broccoli spears or whole green beans
dressed with lemon butter. A festive but simple dessert can
be made from poached fresh or canned pears in raspberry
sauce. Work fresh or frozen berries in the blender with a
spoonful of Triple Sec and a dash of honey. Top with
whipped cream.

Green Peppers

6 large green peppers
2 c. vegetable stock

Filling:
1/4 c. butter
1 c. chopped onion
1 c. sliced fresh mushrooms
salt and pepper
2 t. marjoram
1 T. minced fresh parsley
1 T. Dijon-style mustard
1 egg, slightly beaten
1/2 c. dry whole wheat bread crumbs
1/2 c. ground almonds

2 t. arrowroot

Slice tops from peppers, reserving for another use. Remove seeds and white ribs. Place in shallow baking pan with about 2 cups vegetable stock. Prepare filling by melting butter in 9-inch skillet, saute onion about 3 minutes, add mushrooms and saute another 2 minutes. Remove from heat, add remaining ingredients and combine well. Divide among the peppers. Top each with a large pat of butter and bake in preheated 375 degree oven about 25 minutes, peppers should still be a bit crisp. Remove to warm serving platter. Dissolve arrowroot in about a tablespoon of cold water, stir into stock in baking dish. Place on moderate heat on top of stove and simmer gently, stirring all the while, until sauce thickens, about 2 minutes. Taste for seasoning, pour over peppers on platter and serve.

GO WITHS: Waldorf salad with raisins, walnuts and cubed Feta cheese. Dress with freshly-made garlic mayonnaise (see Appendix). For dessert, a quick eggless mousse (see Appendix).

Potato Surprise

An adaptation of Cordon Bleu, a dish well-suited to a buffet, as are so many of these stuffed vegetables.

6 very large potatoes, baked
1/4 c. butter
1 c. sliced mushrooms
2 T. minced scallions
salt and white pepper
1 t. marjoram
6 soft-boiled eggs, shelled
1/2 c. grated Parmesan
1/2 c. soft bread crumbs
2 T. minced fresh parsley

Take a thin slice off the top of each potato, scoop out leaving shell intact. Place potato in mixing bowl and mash while still hot, adding enough butter to make smooth. Season. In a small skillet, melt butter and saute mushrooms and scallions with seasonings and marjoram just until limp, about 3 minutes. Place an egg in each potato shell and divide mushrooms among the shells. Put mashed potato into a piping bag fitted with a No. 8 or No. 9 rosette tip and pipe potato in rings on top of the filling, beginning at the outside edge. If a pastry bag isn't available, heap in with small spatula making a point in the middle. Combine bread crumbs and Parmesan, distribute over potatoes. Place in buttered baking dish and run under broiler a few minutes to brown lightly. Sprinkle with parsley before serving.

GO WITHS: Pearl onions and thick carrot slices, parboiled and then threaded on 8-inch bamboo skewers alternating with squares of green pepper, cherry tomatoes and small slices of zucchini. Bake or broil quickly to heat through, serve hot with a dipping sauce of Chinese sesame oil, finely-minced ginger root, garlic and soy sauce. A salad of fruited coleslaw made by adding fresh oranges and pineapple to shredded cabbage, dressed with sour cream. For dessert, fudgy brownies.

Appendix
Basic Recipes

Dressings

Mayonnaise

1 egg, large
1 T. wine vinegar
salt and pepper
1 t. Dijon-style mustard
1 c. vegetable or olive oil

Place egg in a blender or food processor and add vinegar, seasoning and mustard. Put lid on and work at highest speed to the count of ten, then pour oil through feed tube in a slow, steady stream. Stop motor as soon as all oil has been poured in. If mixture is too thick, add a few drops of vinegar and stir in by hand. If mixture hasn't thickened properly and looks curdled, pour out into measuring cup and begin again with another egg. This frequently happens if the egg is small. Pour curdled mixture through feed tube as you did the plain oil before. Taste for seasoning.

VARIATIONS:

Garlic: Add 1 large clove, peeled and sliced to base of egg, seasoning and mustard. Motor will incorporate it thoroughly.

Mustard: Increase quantity of mustard to 1 T.

Spiced: Stirring with spoon, add to finished mayonnaise the following: 1/2 t. crushed tarragon, 1 T. fresh minced parsley, 1 T. minced green tops of scallion, 1 T. minced sour pickle.

Vinaigrette

Basic Light:

> 3 T. imported olive oil
> 1 T. white champagne vinegar
> salt and white pepper
> 1 T. minced fresh parsley

Combine all ingredients in small jar with tight fitting lid and shake vigorously. Shake again just before pouring over salad as it is about to be served.

VARIATIONS:

Strong: As above but use 1 1/2 T. red wine vinegar.

Herbed: As in Basic Light dressing, but add 1/2 T. crushed tarragon and 1 T. finely-minced green scallion or chives.

Mustard: As in Basic Strong but add 1 T. Dijon mustard.

Sauces

Brown Sauce

1 T. soy sauce
1 T. miso paste (soy bean paste)
2 T. cornstarch
1 c. water

Combine all ingredients in small saucepan and bring to a
boil over moderate heat. Stir constantly; sauce will
thicken in 2-3 minutes. Keep warm until ready to use.

Tomato Sauce

2 T. olive oil
1 c. chopped onion
3 minced cloves garlic
1 1/2 c. minced green pepper
3 c. chopped tomatoes, fresh or canned
1 t. thyme
salt and pepper

Heat olive oil in 2-quart saucepan over moderate heat.
Saute onion, garlic and pepper about 5 minutes until
tender. Add tomatoes and seasonings. Reduce heat and
simmer gently at least half an hour. Sauce may be made
ahead of time and reheated; it may also be frozen.

White Sauce (Bechamel)

2 c. milk
4 black peppercorns
1 large parsley stem
1 bay leaf
1 slice onion
dash powdered mace
3 T. butter
3 1/2 T. unbleached flour

Scald milk in small saucepan with the seasonings. Set aside to infuse and cool about 10 minutes. Melt butter in another small saucepan, remove from heat and stir in flour with wire whisk. Gradually add milk, leaving behind the seasoning ingredients. Stir smooth and return to moderate heat, stirring constantly with the whisk until sauce thickens, about 5 minutes. If sauce is too thick, add more milk. Consistency should be light and flowing but thick enough to coat a spoon.

Sauce may be made hours ahead or even a day or two before and kept in the refrigerator or it may be frozen. If sauce is to stand more than a few minutes before using, place wax paper, plastic wrap or foil directly on its surface to take up the skin.

Cheese Sauce (Mornay)

1 recipe White Sauce (see above)
3/4 c. grated sharp Cheddar

As soon as white sauce has thickened sufficiently, stir in cheese. Turn off heat and allow cheese to melt in. Sauce should be handled in the same way as white sauce.

Desserts

Gingerbread

1 c. whole wheat flour
1 t. cinnamon
1/4 t. ground cloves
3/4 t. baking soda
1 c. honey
1 egg, large
2 T. minced crystallized ginger
2 T. butter
1/3 c. boiling water

Sift dry ingredients together thoroughly. Combine honey, egg, and butter with boiling water in another bowl, stirring until all are combined and butter and honey have melted. Stir liquid mixture into dry mixture in two batches, combining well. Pour into greased and floured 8-inch square baking pan and bake in preheated 350 degree oven about 25 minutes or until cake comes away from the sides of the pan and the middle rebounds to the touch. Cool 5 minutes in the pan on a rack, then remove from pan and finish cooling on the rack. You can also serve the cake warm with custard sauce.

Custard Sauce

2 c. milk
1-inch vanilla bean, slit lengthwise
3 T. honey
3 egg yolks

Scald milk in small, heavy saucepan or top of double boiler with the vanilla bean. Allow milk to cool with the vanilla about 10 minutes. Remove skin from milk and the vanilla pods. Using a whisk, beat in honey to dissolve in the lukewarm milk, then beat in the yolks one by one. Return saucepan to heat and cook over very gentle heat, stirring constantly until mixture coats a spoon and has thickened lightly. Serve warm over cake or fruit. If you prefer to serve the sauce at room temperature or cold, cover surface with wax paper to absorb the skin which will form on top.

Pound Cake Cordon Bleu

6 oz. butter, room temperature
3/4 c. sugar or 1/3 c. honey
3 large eggs
1 2/3 c. unbleached flour
1 t. baking powder

Work butter light and fluffy in mixing bowl or in food processor. Gradually beat in sugar until mixture has the consistency of whipped cream. Beat in eggs one by one. Sift flour once with baking powder and again into mixing bowl, gradually folding in only enough to combine. Scrape batter into greased and floured 8 x 4-inch loaf pan and bake in preheated 350 degree oven about 45 minutes or until cake has come away from the sides of the pan and rebounds to the touch of a finger in the middle. Remove from pan and cool on wire rack.

Zabaglione

2 eggs
1 t. sugar
2 T. Marsala wine

For each person, beat 2 eggs in a deep mixing bowl over a saucepan of water not quite boiling. Gradually beat in a spoonful of sugar for each portion, then 2 T. Marsala wine. Eggs will become very pale and thick and fluffy. Turn out into champagne glasses and serve quickly before it begins to fall.

Chocolate Mousse

1/2 c. evaporated milk
3/4 c. melted semi-sweet chocolate

Put milk in freezer until very cold, but not frozen solid. Beat to consistency of whipped cream. Combine with melted chocolate. Allow to chill 1-2 hours before serving.

Imperial Rice

Triple Sec, sufficient to cover fruits
1/2 c. diced peaches
1/2 c. diced apricots
1/2 c. diced pineapple
1 c. whipped cream
3 c. creamy rice pudding

In Triple Sec, marinate fruits for about 1 hour. Drain and fold most of fruit into whipped cream and rice pudding. Save some fruit for garnish.

Pack into an oiled melon or tower mold and chill 2-3 hours. Turn out onto cold platter and garnish with remaining fruit and whipped cream rosettes if you wish. The marinade may be passed separately as a sauce.

°°

Index

95